Thanks to those of you who contributed thought or encouragement to this.

I thought I would at least mention you here since I stole some of your thoughts and didn't pay you anything! My wife, Barbara; my daughter, Karis (who encouraged me by laughing at everything I wrote – even though she's 3 and didn't get any of it); the following people from my Fall '07 Youth Culture class: Will Boyd, Mark Centurion, Bethany Cetti, Casey Groves, Joshua Kellogg, Lauren Markling, Daniel Pellegrini, Mallory Smith (thanks for sharing your points of view...and for proving some of mine!); and lastly, to Josh Griffin (who some people think has a better sense of humor than me – dang it!).

Table of Contents

Introduction

Thanks for picking up this book! Whether you're a senior in high school, a freshman in college, or just looking to make the most of your college years, you've come to the right place. This book was written with you in mind. It's full of valuable tips and insights that will help make your college years a little easier and a lot more enjoyable!

The author, Chuck Bomar, has worked with college-age people for over eight years and at one time stood in your shoes with the same questions, problems, struggles, and anxiety about college that you may be facing. Chuck has taken his experience and learnings from the past several years and put them together in this easy-to-read book to help you through this transition. Good luck on the road ahead!

Life Direction

Everyone has pressures put on them, some more serious than others, and different ones depending on our stage of life (like younger guys to let their pants sag, while older guys seem to have pressure to pull up their pants higher and higher above their waist). Every stage of life has unique pressures and for you, one of the biggest is probably trying to find a career path. The pressure to figure this out can be intense. Parents and society drive us to find a direction, but it's just not that easy. A question you may be asking is, "How am I supposed to know what direction I'm going to go when I don't even know what I want!?" If you're experiencing this pressure, here are six things that you should read:

1. The process of discovering what you want to do should be taken slowly.

There is no rush, no matter who keeps asking you. The worst thing you can do is rush into a career path that you hate, simply to satisfy immediate pressures placed on you. I once knew a guy who for 13 years watched a machine put the caps on soda bottles. Yeah, the machine did all the work and he just watched it do its thing. I know this may be a shock to you, but this wasn't his dream job. He got stuck. You will regret settling for something less than you want.

2. Discovering who you are before you try to figure out what you'll do is extremely important.

You have a lot of questions to answer about yourself and what you believe. Take your time. Thinking through this before you get into a career path is your biggest priority. Who are you beyond your life in high school, or now in your college-age years? We all know the 44-year-old guy who still lives off the identity of his high school football days. You must move beyond high school, but you must also move slowly. Jumping too fast in a direction may someday result in "a mid-life crisis." Take your time and seriously work through it now. It will save you a lot of pain later.

3. Finding a temporary job until you find your career is not a bad thing.

We all have responsibilities, and developing different types of skills will add credibility to your work history. But make sure you continue the process of finding out who you are, what you want, and how you're uniquely talented. This will help you think through vocations that fit you, rather than you trying to fit a particular vocation. If you try to fit a vocation, you won't accomplish much at all. Dream big.

4. Working with the right people is vital.

You can actually have job responsibilities you don't care for and yet enjoy your job if you work with the right people. The opposite is also true – you can learn a lot from people who you don't want to be like. But in these situations you have to have skin thicker than the Great Wall of China. And since few of us do, we end up becoming miserable.

5. Find peace in the fact that God already knows what you're going to do *(Acts 17:24-27)*. You can remind your parents of that too!

6. Do not be anxious about tomorrow for it will worry about itself *(Matthew 6:34).*

The key for you is to be faithful today. Taking care of your responsibilities today is more than enough work. Don't be deceived into thinking God will give you direction for your entire life if you're not being faithful with what He asks of you today. It's normal during our college-age years to be expert worriers when it comes to the future, but try to be an expert in faithfulness today. We must be faithful in the small things before God trusts us to be faithful with larger responsibilities *(Luke 16:10).*

SCRIPTURE
Acts 17:24-27; Matthew 6:34; Luke 16:10

Thoughts on Intimacy

As we get older our idea of intimacy begins to change. It becomes much deeper than sex (I promise you this is true), physical interaction (not taking anything away from it, of course), or even dating relationships (no doubt). It's about getting to know another person at a deeper level and allowing them to know who you really are. You now have this desire more than ever so there are five things you need to know regarding intimacy:

1. True intimacy requires vulnerability.

I've always told people there are levels of intimacy with your spouse. Your level of intimacy with your spouse depends largely on how vulnerable you choose to be with her/him. It's one thing to share what you're passionate about, or even what goals or dreams you may have for your lives together. But it's another thing to share the hurts and the struggles you may have, or the sin and temptation that you deal with on a day-to-day basis. In all honesty, this is extremely difficult, but in order to fulfill your desire for intimate relationships you must be willing to share your innermost self. Taking small steps in this direction now is vital. True intimacy moves beyond talking about ethical issues or connecting with someone through an online network. Any relationship that doesn't require you to reveal every part of yourself isn't truly intimate.

2. Your desire for intimacy can lead to problems.

When you have true intimacy with people you will also have more conflict. As weird as it may sound, this is a good thing. If there are no problems in a relationship it usually means one or both of the people involved are not being honest. During your college-age years you will have less immature "high school

drama," but expect relational drama. It's different, but still there.

3. God designed us for intimacy.

You're created for close-knit relationships, so don't rob yourself of that desire. We should first be in close relationship with God and secondly with other people *(Matthew 22:37-40)*. God created us to love Him and love others. It's His command, too. Remember, true love is intimate. We cannot say we love anyone (including God) unless there is intimacy. God already sees you for who you really are; why not acknowledge it?

notes

Intimacy is about getting to know another person at a deeper level and allowing them to know who you really are.

4. When you open yourself up to another person for the possibility of an intimate relationship, you may get hurt.

But it's worth it in the long run. Don't rob yourself of experiencing true intimacy.

5. There is NO risk in a truly intimate relationship with God.

He's seen you at your best and at your worst. Honestly, vulnerability with God has zero risk.

99 Thoughts for College-Age People

Copyright © 2008 Simply Youth Ministry

Simply Youth Ministry
26981 Vista Terrace, Unit C
Lake Forest, CA 92630

www.simplyyouthministry.com

ISBN 978-0-7644-6215-3

Printed in the United States of America

99 Thoughts

for college-age people

insightful tips for life after high school

By Chuck Bomar

Unknown Common Denominators

We face some issues during our college-age years that seem unique to us, but they're actually pretty common for all of our peers. The truth is, you're not alone. Here are a few things you should read to remind you that you're not alone:

Intimidation

It's hard to have all your friends disperse into their own lives, leaving you alone in yours. It can be exciting to move on in our lives, but it's also a bit intimidating. Paranoia might even be a good word to describe the feelings you're having or have had. But just like your sixth-grade fears of getting canned, this intimidation phase always comes to an end. You will develop new relationships and even though it may not seem possible, these new friends will probably be closer than any other before! You might keep in touch with one or two of your high school friends, but this may be from a distance. You will now begin to find friends who will walk with you closely throughout the rest of your life. Want to see if I'm right? Ask some married people about the friends who were in their wedding, and I would be willing to bet few were friends from high school.

Loneliness

You will lose contact with most of your old friends and acquaintances during the first year after graduating from high school. On top of this you will most likely feel disconnected from your parents – mainly because you tried to gain an independence from them in high school. Expect to feel a little lonely. You may feel like you have nobody to talk to, especially when you're in the Taco Bell drive-thru at 4am with nobody in your passenger seat. It intensifies when you're trying to figure out who you are, what direction you're headed, and what areas of your life need growth. In these times here are four things you need to remember:

1. You're not alone.

Pretty much everyone goes through this after high school at some level. Feelings of depression and isolation are completely normal. Hang in there; this will pass.

2. This is a natural process God brings us through to realize who we are and how He's made us unique from everyone else.

3. It's a great time for God to teach you that no matter who leaves, He's always there *(Matthew 28:20)*.

SCRIPTURE

Matthew 28:20

4. You'll go nuts if you keep your thoughts to yourself.

Trust me, there's someone who would love to talk to you. Just ask someone to talk. If you don't know where to go, find a local church, walk in, and simply say, "I need to talk to a pastor."

Re-evaluation

At some point we all re-evaluate the assumptions that defined the early years of our lives. Most people do this during their first couple years after graduating from high school. Everyone will inevitably question their beliefs, possibly to a point of doubting them entirely. This is normal, and actually healthy. There's a lot to think through. Here are eight thoughts about this inevitable process:

1. Don't feel guilty for having doubts.

This process is healthy, even if it feels like your world is falling apart! Most people have doubts about their faith from time to time, but many people won't admit it. You and I aren't the only ones to have doubts; it's totally normal.

2. Things that once seemed black and white to you may all of the sudden be turning grey.

This is simply because you can think at much deeper levels than you ever could before.

3. If things are becoming more complex in your world, it's a sign that you're growing up.

You are realizing things aren't as simple as they used to seem!

4. If confusion is creeping into your life it's because you don't actually know as much as you thought you did.

We all get blindsided by this truth at some point. Don't throw in the towel. Just learn more!

5. Truth has nothing to hide, so ask your questions and share your doubts with someone you trust.

tip

Go to someone who really knows Scripture.

6. Just because things seem much more complex, it doesn't mean your faith is wrong.

And it certainly doesn't mean your faith is dying. It just means you're maturing and thinking through things you never have before. Your faith will become stronger when it's challenged.

7. Re-evaluating your beliefs will allow you to have a faith of your own.

During your college-age years, you will move past living off your parents' beliefs. This means you need to examine the beliefs you were taught and determine if you truly believe them for yourself. Babies are weaned off their mom's milk, and this is your weaning process.

8. Just because someone caused you to think in a new way about your faith doesn't mean they are right.

There may be very logical and biblical responses to whatever that person said. Scripture may even clearly show their thoughts to be wrong. Don't trust other people's thoughts over God's. Make sure you're comparing everything people say to what God says *(Acts 17:11)*.

> SCRIPTURE
>
> *Acts 17:11*

Roommate Etiquette

Living with different people can be a ton of fun, but it can also become a nightmare. You will likely have several different roommate arrangements before you get married. There are things that everyone tries that never seem to work out. So, here are some practical thoughts for living with other people:

1. Make sure you buy a hamper
that seals tightly – there's nothing worse than a room that smells like dirty clothes (especially when three or four people are living in a 10x10 dorm room).

2. "Community food" never works.

Buy your own food and mark it! Treat every meal as your last. The plate you eat off might be the only thing your roommates won't steal.

3. Oatmeal, rice, potatoes, pasta, peanut butter and jelly sandwiches, and the infamous Top Ramen can give you a solid three meals a day. And it's pretty inexpensive too.

4. Wash your sheets!

When you can pull off your comforter and see where you lay down at night, it's too late.

tip

Taking a shower before you go to bed will add at least a week before sheets need to be washed.

5. There always seems to be at least one person we live with who thinks it's totally appropriate to walk around completely naked.

Just remember, there's nothing worse than being "that" person.

6. Guys, more cologne doesn't cover up bad hygiene.

It doesn't matter how expensive it was.

7. Economy-size Advil bottles will come in handy!

It will help those headaches caused by professors or snoring roommates. If your roommate snores, maybe drop a few of these in his/her mouth in the middle of the night.

8. If you live in a dorm make sure to wear flip-flops in the shower.

If you don't, you will definitely get fungus at some point. If you already have fungus, as a prank, make sure to NOT wear flip flops. Then sell everyone else the anti-fungal cream for profit. Just kidding. Kind of.

9. Drying your clothes to get wrinkles out doesn't mean they're clean – even if you throw dryer sheets in!

10. Having a weekly time where you and your roommates hang out together will really keep unity in the house.

It can also serve as a time to talk through house issues. But most importantly use this time to just hang out and laugh.

Money Wisdom

Money has always been a huge source of problems in our world *(1 Timothy 6:10)*. People don't realize how much they love the freedom it brings. In other words, money can allow us to do a lot of things we enjoy. But without even knowing it these things we once viewed as freedoms can quickly become burdens. Money can ruin our lives and actually hold us back if we're not careful. Most adults in financial trouble link their problems back to poor decisions they made during their college-age years. So, here are nine thoughts in regards to money:

1. Focusing on immediate pleasures versus thinking from a long-term perspective will bring problems.

Your tendency will be to focus on immediate things. Be very careful.

2. The most money you will spend will be on food.

> **tip**
>
> If you live on campus use the DC [Dining Commons] card you **ALREADY** paid for.

3. You'll tend to spend money you don't have (i.e. using your credit cards when you can't pay the bill).

I know it's much easier (and fun!) to do the things you want, but charging it now will only end in regret later.

4. Warning: Cups of coffee add up!

Plus you don't want to build up too strong of a tolerance toward caffeine; you'll need it during finals week.

5. As lame as it sounds, living on a budget will save you a lot of headaches.

God has given you a certain amount of money, so spend it wisely. Don't spend more than He's given you. In a sense, overspending is a way of saying we're not content with what He's provided.

6. Buy your books online.

It's much cheaper than at the bookstore. Also, attend classes a couple times before you purchase the book – you may not even read it.

7. The first check you should write every month should be a tithe check to a local church.

This way you're not only being faithful, you also get reminded of what takes priority. The second check can be to Taco Bell for a combo #2 – unless you already paid for a DC card!

24

8. Calling the 800 number on the back of your ATM card to verify your balance doesn't mean your checkbook is balanced!

9. Buying things like a motorcycle, boat, or nicer car may seem like luxuries now, but these will eventually become responsibilities.

What you think is freedom can turn into bondage if you're not careful.

notes

Did you know most adults in financial trouble link their problems back to poor decisions they made during their college-age years?

Getting a college education is important in American culture. There are some very good things about pursuing an education, but here are nine things you should read regarding this pursuit:

1. We ought to be getting an education for the purpose of becoming a missionary in a particular field of work, not to just make more money.

The more you excel in a job the more you can naturally reach out to your co-workers. Every missionary prepares for the field. They learn what it's like, how things function, and where they fit in. Seek to have this perspective of your education.

notes

It's never worth it to fail a class.

2. There's no rush to get through school.

Be open to the thought that there's more to life than succeeding in American culture. Maybe God would have you go overseas for a year or two before you pursue an education. You can always get a degree, but you can't always get up and go on the mission field. You may want to consider this. Life only gets busier.

3. The Schaffer method will never be used again!

Learn it because you have to, but know you'll never use it again. If you don't know what the Schaffer method is, you just proved my point!

4. It's never worth it to fail a class.

If you lack discipline in this area you will definitely regret it; everyone does. What people don't realize is that life just requires you to be even more disciplined later – yes, it's going to be harder. Get through it now and save yourself a lot of headaches.

5. Going to a community college doesn't make you behind in life; it just allows you to get the same general education at a cheaper rate!

6. One of the biggest areas that can cause people to question their faith in college is science. There are three things you need to know about science:

 a. Science does not determine truth. It does, however, sometimes find it. The world has defined science as the instrument that determines truth, but Scripture says that God is the One to define what truth is *(Psalm 31:5, 111:7; John 14:6).*

 b. The definition of science is man's observations of creation. Man is flawed, biased, and has agendas. Scientists will even tell you they cannot be completely

SCRIPTURE

Psalm 31:5, 111:7; John 14:6

objective in their research. Very little if anything we do as human beings is purely objective, so use discernment when it comes to "scientific facts." Not every one of them is in fact true.

c. Science doesn't necessarily contradict your faith. If someone observing creation finds truth, it's God's truth. Because it's God's truth and you are God's, that means it's your truth. Claim it *(1 Corinthians 3:18-23)*! Don't let science or anyone else claim God's truth as theirs.

7. Another area that causes people to doubt their faith is philosophy courses. Here are four things you need to know about philosophy:

a. Philosophy is simply human beings trying to intellectually make sense of the world. Like science, this is biased and cannot be separated from personal agendas.

b. Secular philosophy doesn't always contradict your faith.

c. Although someone's thought processes might make sense, it doesn't make them correct. People are not smarter than God – even if they think they are. Always compare what you hear to Scripture.

> **tip**
>
> You will need to know more Scripture to discern through these things, so you have to study.

d. Be careful to not throw your faith away just because someone made what seemed like a logical argument against it *(1 Corinthians 3:18-23)*. It may not be as logical as you initially think, especially from a biblical perspective.

> SCRIPTURE
>
> *1 Corinthians 3:18-23*

8. Using a semi-colon means both sides of the sentence must stand on its own.

Trust me; you'll use this one!

9. Don't get too caught up in your major; you'll probably change it anyway.

If you're reading this as a 5th or 6th year senior and still haven't landed on a major, here's a tip: write out a list of majors, pin them against the wall, and throw a dart. Run with the one it lands closest to. By now you've probably accumulated too many loans to not finish school…you need to have something to show for the debt (hopefully not too much debt!).

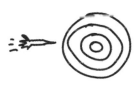

Random Daily Life "Wisdom"

As we go through life we experience realities that we never expected. Some things are more serious than others, but we all have things we've learned over time. So, here are a few random thoughts regarding your daily life as a college-age person:

1. Drying your clothes doesn't mean they're clean!

2. The world does not revolve around you.

Embracing this today will save you a lot of frustration tomorrow when things don't go the way you wanted.

3. "The freshman 15" is real.

4. Don't be intimidated by people.

People are like spiders: they're more afraid of you than you are of them.

5. Some people are like dogs, too: they'll be your best friend as long as you feed them, but the next thing you know they're peeing all over your stuff.

Serving people is good, but enabling a con-artist is another. Serve, don't enable.

6. The first year or so after graduating from high school is often a time of loneliness for people.

Remember that feelings of detachment are absolutely normal, but this will change! Hang in there.

7. In another 25 years you will recognize God's way is best, so you might as well try to live that way now.

Plus, in another 60 years or so, you'll be with Him.

8. Stop and smell the roses every once in a while.

Don't be in such a rush.

9. You most likely won't be able to afford new clothes, so ask for them on birthdays and Christmas.

10. Most things in life aren't as big of a deal as we make them.

We tend to emotionally react to things that don't really matter in the long run. If it won't impact your life 10 years from now, it's not that big of a deal.

11. When you go home for the holidays expect to be:

a. Lonely because not all your friends come home, and your dog may have died and no one told you about it.

b. Frustrated with your parents. You've changed, but they haven't. Plus they're now realizing how much money you really cost them!

c. Ready to leave three days before you're supposed to. Next time shoot for a five-day visit instead of 10. Seriously. Tell your boss you want to work. This way you have an excuse to not stay as long, and your parents will think you're just learning to be responsible.

d. Pressured by your parents to spend time with them when all you want to do is spend time with your friends.

But remember, they're probably the ones paying (or helping to pay) your college bills.

12. Drinking games are overrated.

13. Know that spontaneity will often override discipline in your life.

But this is usually not good. Giving into this too much will cause regrets later in life.

14. You're not above working.

Working a menial job is better than not having one at all.

15. You're not as smart as you think you are.

It seems like people that are actually smart realize this (I think that's why it's so hard for me).

16. You will begin to see and recognize all your weaknesses.

Don't be discouraged, you're not as bad as you think you might be.

17. Your close friends will help you find out where you need to grow, but won't always give you the best advice on how.

Seek older people's advice.

18. You think you're busy now, but there will come a day when you will realize you weren't really busy at all.

When you talk about how stressed you are and older people just smile or laugh – yep, that's what they're thinking.

19. Staying up all night to hang out with friends doesn't make you too busy to follow through with commitments, even though you'll use that excuse.

Identity

Your self-identity will drive everything in your life. You will find that everything in life is an identity issue shaped by the way you answer the question "Who am I?" It seems like a simple question to answer, but unfortunately for many of us it's not. You will search for an identity in something. It's part of how God designed us. There are all kinds of different ways we try to define ourselves, but here are at least six unhealthy areas where you may find yourself trying to seek your identity:

1. In Crowds.

As Christians we claim to have a personal relationship with Jesus Christ. This is the one thing that really sets us apart from any other religion. A lot of people say they have a relationship with Christ, but when examined the reality is there isn't much of one at all. Their "relationship" really doesn't exist outside of religious gatherings. A question you should ask yourself is: How much of my "relationship with Christ" happens apart from any formal gathering? Take all the youth group gatherings away, and what is your relationship with Christ like? When you're alone is there really a relationship? Your identity must move beyond religious gatherings.

2. In Sin.

The number one ingredient to a mediocre Christian life is wrongfully identifying ourselves in sin struggles, rather than in Christ. Right now you are becoming aware of your weaknesses. Be very careful. As you search for an identity in something, you may embrace it in your sin struggles. These struggles cause many to shrink back from truly pursuing a relationship with Christ and engaging in ministry. Remind yourself of your Identity in Christ and His righteousness. You are holy and blameless before God, my friend *(Ephesians 1:3-5)*. Let that define you.

3. In Circumstances.

Too often, we build our faith on circumstances. These can be in a job, wealth, painful times, loneliness, clothes we wear, or cars we drive. Unfortunately, circumstances always change, leaving us in search of another identity. This is when we find ourselves in an identity crisis. Finding your identity and hope in the One who will never change is vital *(Hebrews 13:8)*!

4. In Society.

You can easily gain a sense of identity in social status. The company that hires us or the size of our paycheck can give us a status

SCRIPTURE

Ephesians 1:3-5
Hebrews 13:8

in society. Finding an identity in these types of things is dangerous. Your life is filled with unknowns right now, so it's far too easy to place our hope in a job offer or a certain salary. However, our career dreams can change, or they may get crushed. You must not allow society to define you. Your identity goes far beyond the things of this world *(1 Peter 2:11)*. Doesn't it seem shallow to allow what we do for a living to define who we are as a person? There's something much deeper, much more real, and much more meaningful.

5. In the American Dream.

Owning a home and having a family is what we consider the American Dream. We have to understand, however, that the American definition of a successful life is not necessarily God's idea. Many times it's exactly opposite. The standards of our culture shouldn't define

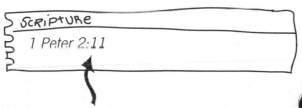

SCRIPTURE

1 Peter 2:11

you. The standards of your parents shouldn't define you either. Be content with whatever God has given you in Christ, brought your way, or given you to do. Our dream should be to embrace our true identity in Christ, not what America says is important.

6. In a Relationship.

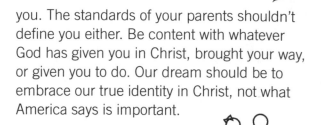

You know those people that always seem to have a girlfriend or boyfriend? They may rarely recognize it, but this is a major identity issue. It's so easy to seek an identity in a relationship with someone else. The problem is that relationships typically come to an end. Who will you be when it ends? Who defines you?

notes

You will search for an identity in something. It's part of how God designed us.

Faith

At this point in your life, you are probably gaining an entirely different perspective of the word "faith." Good. So many times growing up, our perspective isn't accurate. Here are some things you need to know when it comes to your Christian faith:

1. Enjoying life is God's desire for us, but make sure you're living in light of eternity *(Ecclesiastes 11:9).*

2. Being honest with all the ways you are re-evaluating your faith is a must.

No more playing the "church game." If you have questions or doubts, just be honest about them. There are answers to each of your questions (read *John 14:1-7* to see Thomas' interaction with Jesus).

3. Remember that truth has nothing to hide, so search it out *(Matthew 7:7)*.

4. Cling to a local church.

That's not the typical choice for most people your age. No Christian school or campus organization compares to being connected to a church family!

5. Having an older, more mature mentor is vital.

They can save you from making some major mistakes, and learning about the ones they made will help you get where you want to be faster than you could alone.

SCRIPTURE
Ecclesiastes 11:9; John 14:1-7;
Matthew 7:7

6. Always remember that *who* you are spiritually matters more than *who* others say you should be, or *what* they say you should do. Embracing your spiritual identity must be the highest priority for you. Never let someone or something other than God define you.

7. Don't wait to see a burning bush before you take steps of faith.

If you do, you'll never move.

8. Relying on feelings and emotions always leads to a sense of hopelessness.

However, relying on what you know to be true about God always leads to hope *(Psalm 42:5)*.

9. The Christian faith is just that: a life of faith.

> SCRIPTURE
>
> *Psalm 42:5; Colossians 2:20-23*

Don't reduce it to religious routine *(Colossians 2:20-23)*. Be careful of reducing an authentic Christian life to a set of rules. Get it? I said, "Don't say don't." Ha. If you didn't get it, never mind.

10. Reading your Bible,
going to church, and abstaining from drugs, alcohol, and premarital sex don't make you right in the eyes of God.

Our faith is much deeper than that *(Romans 3:28)*.

11. If someone says **something that causes you to question your faith, it doesn't make your faith wrong *(1 Corinthians 3:18-19; Colossians 2:8)*.**

SCRiPTURE

Romans 3:28; 1 Corinthians 3:18-19; Colossians 2:8

12. Read your Bible one paragraph at a time, soak it in, and live it out.

Reading more is not necessarily better. If you can't think through and live out what you've read, it was useless.

13. If you get bored reading Scripture or going to church, it's probably because you're not living out what you're reading or learning.

Following Scripture can be difficult, but it's certainly not boring.

14. The Bible has nothing to hide.

Ask your questions.

15. The Bible wasn't just written by a bunch of men.

That argument against its credibility is
shallow and based on a fundamental
misunderstanding of God *(2 Timothy 3:16)*.

SCRIPTURE

2 Timothy 3:16

Wisdom on Campus Ministries

1. You will be exposed to different perspectives of the Christian faith – definitely different from the way you were raised.

This will cause you to re-evaluate your beliefs and possibly doubt all you know. This is okay. Growing up in church can shelter us from these differences. Be prepared for that shelter to be ripped off – if it hasn't been already.

2. Involvement in a college-age ministry will help you understand that you don't know as much as you think you do.

3. But being involved in a campus ministry can cause you to lose touch with a local church.

This causes problems when you graduate; where will you connect then? Stay connected to a local church. Use your gifts to serve the church as well. Otherwise, transitioning after graduation will be much more difficult.

4. These ministries are usually good at evangelism, but not necessarily discipleship.

This is where a local church can be very helpful to you.

5. Small groups are often led by students.

Be wise; this can be the blind leading the blind.

Connecting with New People

Getting new friends at college always happens, but here are some ideas that may help you get to know people more quickly:

1. Making good friends takes time.

Be patient and don't rush it. You don't want to be known as the "needy one."

2. Get involved in a ministry on campus or in a church.

Make it a priority to go on their first retreat. You will definitely gain some friends.

3. Don't spend too much time checking out different groups.

If you do, you will find yourself wandering forever. Find one that fits best (not perfectly!), and go with it.

4. Get involved in a small group of some sort.

Preferably a spiritual one – and not some Ouija board or voodoo spiritual. I mean getting involved with a group of people who are really striving to see the world from God's perspective.

5. Join a study group in a class where you excel.

This will put you in a position where people will come to you with questions they have.

6. Take a class with a lab; you will have to work with a group.

7. Ask someone if they want to study over a cup of coffee.

And don't just ask cute people of the opposite sex! This might actually hinder you from making more friends.

Dating Wisdom

Dating relationships are a topic you probably think about a lot. One of the questions we always ask ourselves prior to marriage is, "How do I know when the right one comes?" Well, here are some questions and thoughts to help you determine the answer to that:

1. Don't date an idiot, even if they're an extremely good-looking idiot. Period.

2. If your dating relationship doesn't honor God, your marriage probably won't either.

Don't think your partner will change once you're married. I've heard many horror stories from people who thought their spouse would change.

3. You have to marry a person for who they are, NOT what they might be.

Not following this principle may cause your dreams for marriage to end in a nightmare.

4. Dating someone to meet our own needs is unhealthy.

We all long for intimacy with another person and long to have a companion to trust in, but we often lack patience. When this happens, we can date someone just for the sake of dating them. No true passion is involved. No future is possible. But our "needs" are temporarily being met. This is not honoring to ourselves or the person we're dating, and most importantly it's not honoring to God.

5. Questions for women to ask in the dating process:

    a. Can he lead me spiritually?

b. Does he have a ministry? If he doesn't, this should be a red flag. If he can't lead other people in their walk, how do you know that he can lead you? A person who loves God and loves people wants to serve both. A mature believer will either already have or be actively looking for an area of ministry.

c. Does he show genuine concern for my holiness? One way you can answer this quickly is whether or not he protects your purity.

d. Does he challenge me in my walk with God? Does he ask you if you have spent time in the Word? Does he confront you on sinful tendencies? Do his convictions convict you?

e. Do I have any doubt that he is seeking the Lord in everything he does? This is necessary because if you can answer this positively, then you know that he will seek the Lord when it comes to you. That is extremely important!

f. Am I confident that I can follow him in everything? If you can answer the previous question positively, then this one should be answered positively, too.

g. Is it evident that he is caring, and protective of me? This should not be in an obsessive way, but rather in a loving, Christ-like way.

6. Questions for guys to ask:

a. Is she supportive of me and my ministry? If not, you can't expect her to be in marriage.

b. Is she willing to follow me? If not now, you can't count on her to do it later.

c. Is she hot? (Just kidding). Kind of. Almost. Well, you do need to be attracted to the person. Gosh, my wife is hot –

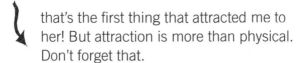

that's the first thing that attracted me to her! But attraction is more than physical. Don't forget that.

d. Is she pursuing goals in her own life that contradict what God is calling me to?

e. Does she respect my decisions even when she disagrees?

7. Questions for everyone to answer in the dating process:

a. Am I preparing to be the right person more than I'm looking for the right person?

b. Is she/he ready to leave the emotional and financial dependency of his/her parents?

c. Do I have an honest desire to get to know his/her heart and mind, and does

he/she have that same desire? Signs for this are: you are excited about spending time with them, and you listen to what they have to say.

d. Do we have true, intimate conversations? Signs for this are: open with each other, talk about "real-life issues," talk about walks with God and confront where necessary, ask questions that expose who the other person is, etc.

e. Is she/he secure in, and have a desire to serve Christ? We know that a Christian should not marry an unbeliever *(2 Corinthians 6:14)*, so it is necessary that this question is answered positively.

f. What can I do to get to the point where I can fulfill my God-designed role?

SCRIPTURE

2 Corinthians 6:14

g. What are two characteristics that I personally should have as a person preparing for marriage?

h. Who can help me grow in this area?

i. What three marriages do I admire, and why do I admire them?

Well, that's it.

I hope those **99 thoughts** will help make your college-age years a little easier to survive. You'll still face plenty of questions, doubts, and difficult times. But I hope these thoughts can be tools and words of encouragement during this exciting time of life. In the next few years, you'll experience moments and events that you'll remember for the rest of your life. So go out and make some awesome memories with your friends and family. Most of all, remember that **God's watching out for you every step of the way!**

99 Thoughts for College-Age People

insightful tips for life after high school

You're embarking on one of the greatest adventures in your life. The transition from high school to the college-age years offers an endless list of new opportunities and experiences. More responsibility. Less time. Major decisions. Heartbreak. Life lessons. Fresh beginnings.

In this humorous and thought-provoking book, **Chuck Bomar** reaches into his bag of life experience and digs up some pearls of wisdom that can help make these years more manageable and more memorable. You'll enjoy discovering these thoughts on your own, or using them to launch some fun discussions with your friends or people in your small group.

However you choose to use this book, you'll be sure to save yourself some pain and money – and maybe even some foot fungus.

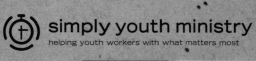

simply youth ministry

helping youth workers with what matters most

ISBN 978-0-7644-6215-3   USD $4.99

9 780764 462153   5 0 4 9 9

Group

Real. **Bold.** Love.

Printed in the U.S.A.

Religion / Christian Ministry / Youth